Eb Alto Saxophone

MASTER SOLOS
by Larry Teal

Edited by Linda Rutherford

Contents

To access companion recorded performances
and accompaniments online, visit:
www.halleonard.com/mylibrary

Enter Code
5282-8122-5254-0980

ISBN 978-0-7935-9549-5

HAL•LEONARD®

Visit Hal Leonard Online at
www.halleonard.com

Contact Us:
Hal Leonard
7777 West Bluemound Road
Milwaukee, WI 53213
Email: info@halleonard.com

In Europe contact:
Hal Leonard Europe Limited
42 Wigmore Street
Marylebone, London, W1U 2RN
Email: info@halleonardeurope.com

In Australia contact:
Hal Leonard Australia Pty. Ltd.
4 Lentara Court
Cheltenham, Victoria, 3192 Australia
Email: info@halleonard.com.au

Andante and Bourrée

musical term

andante   moderate tempo

One of the most well-known composers of the late Baroque period (1600-1750) was George Frederic Handel. Handel was born in Germany and traveled extensively throughout his life. This travel contributed greatly to the international flavor of his compositions. He was a master of the Italian traditions of solo and instrumental music, English choral style, and German contrapuntal techniques. Probably his best known work is the "Messiah" performed during the Christmas and Easter seasons. Handel's flute sonatas are standard literature for flute students of all ages. These two movements, "Andante and Bourree", are from his third sonata for flute.

In each of the solos in this book, you'll see markings like . . . M M ♪ = 84. The M.M. stands for Maelzel's Metronome, the inventor of the metronome. This particular marking means that the metronome should be set at 84 and each click represents the length of an eighth note. Remember the eighth note now gets one beat and the quarter note two. These indications are suggestions of a tempo. If at first you cannot play the solo at this tempo, practice it slower and gradually increase the speed as you learn it. If this tempo is too fast for you and your accompanist to perform well, play it at a speed that is comfortable for both of you.

Playing a wind instrument requires a change in the rhythm of normal breathing. You must take in the breath quickly and release it over a longer period of time. Learning to develop breath support, which is the term used for breath pressure and control, is perhaps the most important factor in producing a fine tone. Since the breath is the only power which makes the reed vibrate, it can make or break your tone quality.

It will help to think of the lungs and waist area as the bottom of a balloon. As air is allowed to escape from the balloon (lungs), the air is forced out by pressure all around the balloon. It is not only the diaphragm muscle that creates breath support, but all of the muscles around your waist area: front, sides, and back.

Try the following steps to develop breath control:
1. Sit or stand straight.
2. Keep chest expanded but immobile.
3. Inhale and think of filling the forward stomach area first, then the sides, and finally the back. At first do this in three steps; later, all at one time and quickly.
4. When exhaling the air stream, you should get the sensation of releasing it, not blowing. This release should be a relaxed feeling.

Play on a full breath when possible, so you will have lots of breath support and a reserve of air for the long phrases. Learn to control the air stream so it is even and to keep the neck and shoulder muscles relaxed. The best tone on the saxophone is produced in a relaxed, but controlled manner.

When you are listening to the solos on your cassette, you'll notice that many of the longer tones seem to "fluctuate" or "pulsate", have a rolling effect. This is called vibrato, a technique used by vocalists, string and wind instrumentalists to make the tone quality warmer and more expressive. It is an essential technique for a good saxophonist, but should be used only after a full, rich tone quality has already been established.

There are different methods of producing the vibrato, but the most used and most successful is obtained by an up and down movement of the lower jaw, somewhat like you would say "ah-ah-ah-etc.". You should practice this without the saxophone at first. Learn to move the jaw evenly in a set rhythm about four pulsations to a beat at MM=60 to start.

PREPARATION 1

ah   ah   ah   ah   ah   ah   ah   ah   ah   ah   ah etc.

Tick   *Tick*   *Tick*

Do this exercise holding a pencil or your finger between the teeth so the lower jaw is down (the mouthpiece will be in this position later). Be sure you are saying the syllable "ah", not "yah" or "wah" because these syllables use the wrong set of muscles. Be sure to hold the corners of your mouth in and the lower lip with plenty of flesh between the lower teeth and the reed. Think of your embouchure as a rubber band surrounding the mouthpiece and reed and do not bite into the reed.

When you are blowing, you do not actually say the word "ah", but the jaw goes through this motion. At first the sound will be rough and unmusical, but at this point, it should be even. Try the exercise below with four pulsations on a beat.

PREPARATION 2

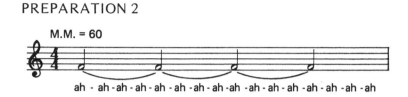

Practice vibrato on just one note until you get the feel of an even, relaxed motion, then try other tones in the middle and upper registers. Now try the following exercise using more than one note.

PREPARATION 3

Narrow the distance the jaw moves to make the pulsations more compact. Be sure the air support is constant.

PREPARATION 4

Use three pulsations for each quarter note in this exercise. The speed will be slightly faster.

PREPARATION 5

3

A number of factors will affect how you use vibrato: the **register** in which you are playing, the **length** of the note, the **intensity** of the note within the phrase, and with what **instruments** you are playing. Listening to the solos on the cassette and other recordings of saxophone solo performances, will give you a better idea of the use of vibrato. There is no set rule for the use of the vibrato, since it is largely a matter of musical taste. As you learn the vibrato, the rate and number of pulsations on a note should suit the length of the tone and the style of the piece. For example, at a metronome marking of ♩=80 there should be about four pulsations to the quarter note. It takes time and practice to acquire a musical vibrato, but you will learn instinctively how and when to use the technique. Whenever it is used, it should be used sparingly and be kept narrow with spinning tone. Try to imitate the human voice.

Measures 1-8   The first part of this solo is slow and lyrical. Notice that the metronome marking is ♪ = 84 so each click is equal to one eighth note or two clicks are equal to one quarter note. Use some vibrato and pay close attention to all articulation and dynamic markings. Be sure to set the tempo in your mind before you begin. You start the solo alone, so your accompanist will pick up the tempo from you. In measure 2 there is a new rhythm using thirty-second notes. A thirty-second note is equal to 1/8 of a quarter note. Practice the following exercise using thirty-second notes in several different rhythmic combinations. Notice that the thirty-seconds occur at different places in measures 2 and 4.

PREPARATION 6

PREPARATION 7

The thirty-second notes come on the second eighth note of measure 2. Put a slight crescendo-decrescendo on this rhythmic figure. You'll notice crescendos and decrescendos within the phrase. The highest dynamic in these should be about "mf". These slight changes of expression are called "nuances" and add color to a composition. Beginning at the end of measure 3, the dynamic level should be slightly louder to contrast with the "piano" level at the beginning. Another group of thirty-seconds appears on the second half of beat 1 in measure 4. Make a difference between the

separated notes and slurred notes in measures 6 and 7. The loudest part of this movement begins on the last note of measure 7 to finish this phrase.

In measure 8 you have a trill, which is a rapid alternation of a note and the scale note above it. This trill should start slowly and gradually speed up. The illustration below shows you how the trill would look written out.

ILLUSTRATION 1

Practice the exercise below for smoothness and evenness of notes. Set the metronome at a slower speed, ♩=60. The beat in each measure is divided into two, three, four, six, and eight equal parts. Try to lift the finger about one-eighth of an inch above the key.

PREPARATION 8

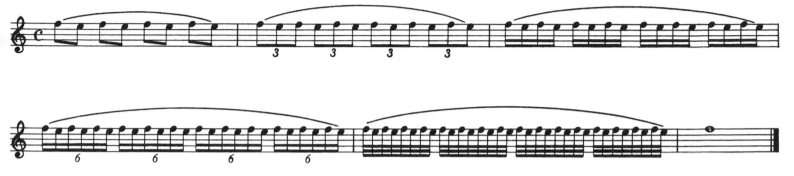

Measures 9-15   The pick-up for measure 9 begins the second part of this movement. In measure 10 the thirty-seconds occur on the second eighth note of the measure. Except for the last measure, this section is a repeat of the first. Put a slight ritard. and diminuendo on the last measure to finish the movement.

musical terms

1st time - *mf*   first time play medium loud
2nd time - *p*   second time play soft

The second movement is a bourree, a lively dance in 2/4 or 4/4 time, and usually beginning with an upbeat or pick-up note. The Baroque composers often used it as one of the faster movements in the sonata.

Measures 1-8   This entire movement should be light and bouncy with crisp staccato. Be sure you are tonguing just the tip of the reed, not the flat underneath part. Remember that "1st time — mf" means the first time it is played "mezzo forte" and "2nd time — p" means that the repeat is "piano". Whenever a section is repeated exactly, it is standard practice to play the repeat at a different dynamic level for contrast.

Whenever a half note occurs on the second beat, put a slight accent on it to emphasize the syncopation.

Measures 9-22   Begin the second section "forte". It is a variation of the original theme starting on a different note. In this section the motive using four eighth notes in sequence is developed. A sequence is a group of notes which are repeated but started on a different note each time. Measures 15 through 22 are sequences each starting one step higher. When you are playing these measures, crescendo gradually to a "forte" in measure 17. The second part of the phrase should begin softly and also crescendo.

On the repeat, ritard. slightly at the end. Again make a contrast in the dynamics when you repeat this section. You should indicate the cut-off of the last note.

Andante and Bourrée
from
Handel Sonata No. III

George Frederic Handel
(1685 - 1759)

Adagio and Allegro

musical term

adagio   slowly

new note

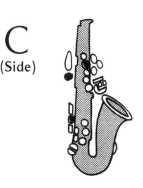

C
(Side)

Frederick the Great, King of Prussia, was an accomplished flutist, composer, and active patron of the arts. He also wrote many compositions in collaboration with other composers, most of whom he kept nameless. Since he lived during the Baroque period of music history (1600-1750), his compositions reflect the style of this period: chromatic, contrasting sections, and changes in rhythms within a composition. Only the bass line was fixed with the chord numbers provided. The performer then embellished the melody above this bass line.

Because the saxophone was not invented until 1840 by Adolph Sax, the saxophone player isn't able to play Baroque music unless he uses transcriptions, special arrangements for the saxophone. These two movements, "Adagio and Allegro", are from one of Frederick the Great's twenty-five flute sonatas.

Measures 1-8   Tonguing should be light but distinct throughout the "Adagio". Be prepared for your entrance in measure 1 by setting your embouchure and fingers and taking a breath in plenty of time. Because you and your accompanist begin together, you should establish the tempo ahead of time. You could indicate one measure of eighth notes before you begin. To actually start the solo, give a cue with a small up-down motion of your instrument.

In measure 3 you have a trill. The illustration below shows measure 3 as it is written and approximately how it should sound. As you will hear on the tape, the trill begins slowly and gradually gets faster.

ILLUSTRATION 2

Practice the exercise below for smoothness and evenness of notes. Set the metronome at a slower speed, ♩=60. The beat in each measure is divided into two, three, four, six, and eight equal parts. Remember to lift the finger only about one eighth of an inch above the key.

PREPARATION 9

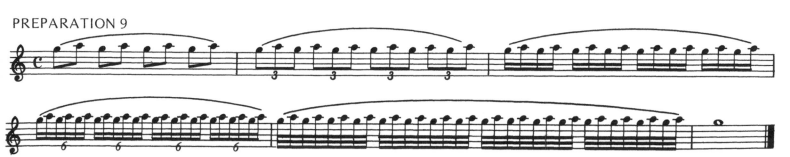

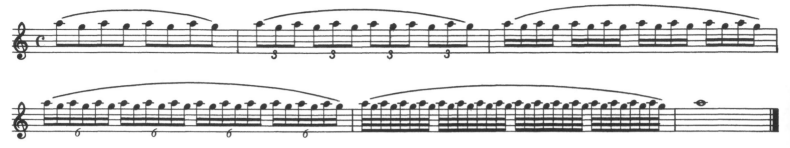

If absolutely necessary you could take a breath in measure 7, but it would be better to play to the end of measure 8 before breathing.

Measures 9-12   The phrase beginning in measure 9 should be a little louder than the first phrase. Remember to keep the tonguing light, but distinct throughout the solo. In measure 12 put a diminuendo on the "C" and "B" to end the phrase. This will keep the sound from ending abruptly.

Measures 12-16 This phrase is again soft. Be sure to keep the rhythm steady. In measure 16 the dotted eighth-sixteenth note pattern is used. Think of the dotted eighth as three tied sixteenth notes. Be sure to hold the dotted eighth for its full length. The following exercise will give you practice playing this rhythmic pattern. Think the rhythm in sixteenth notes, like a "ticker" going in your mind.

PREPARATION 11

Measures 17-24 When moving from the low "D" to the "F", use the quarter rest to prepare for the "F". Think of the pitch of the note, take your breath, and be sure the embouchure is set. The note won't explode if you're prepared. In measure 19 round-off the phrase by putting a slight diminuendo on the "F" to "E".

Start the final phrase softly and gradually crescendo to the last measure. On the second half of beat 2 in measure 23 there is another trill. Practice the trill exercise using the notes of this trill. The side "C" fingering shown above will make this trill easier to play. The forefinger of the right hand should hit the side C lever between the knuckle and the middle joint. Keep the finger close to the key when trilling.

PREPARATION 12

PREPARATION 13

Measure 23 should be played as it is shown below.

ILLUSTRATION 3

"Ritard" slightly on measure 24 and play each note
tongued, full value, and "forte" to finish the movement.

musical terms

allegro   **lively**

ma non troppo   **but not too fast**

Measures 1-14   The second part of this solo, "Allegro",
is faster. The metronome marking is ♩=100, which tells
you that each click now represents the quarter note beat.
Again you indicate the tempo and give a cue to begin. There
should not be a lot of time between movements, so set the
tempo and begin the second movement without much delay.
After you rehearse for a while, the tempos will become more
familiar to you.

In this movement make the contrast of the dynamics very
noticeable. You should also watch the articulations very
carefully and slur only the notes marked. In measure 2
there are two small notes before the first beat. These are
called grace or ornamental notes, decorative pitches that in
this interpretation are played ahead of the beat. The example
below shows how they are written and how they are played.

ILLUSTRATION 4

Try the following exercise for practice playing these grace notes.

PREPARATION 14

Begin measure 5 a little softer than the first phrase. The
trill in measure 13 would look like the illustration below
if it were written out.

ILLUSTRATION 5

Practice the trill exercise using the notes of this trill. Be
sure to go back to the beginning of the "Allegro" for the
repeat.

technique should be used again on the four sixteenth notes
in measure 26. In measures 20 and 22 use the same trill
pattern as in measure 13. Notice that the trill in measure
20 goes to an "F♯", which is indicated by the ♯ after the
abbreviation (tr.).

Measures 15-26   Count very carefully when beginning
this section and don't rush the sixteenth notes. Be sure to
hold the tied eighth notes and sixteenth note for their
full value. In measure 18 put a slight decrescendo on the
"F" to "E" to make the phrase sound finished. This

Measures 27-32   Begin "forte" in this phrase. Then
start the last two sixteenth notes of measure 28 "piano".
Measure 30 should be "forte" to finish the solo. On the
repeat of this section "ritard" slightly at the end.

Adagio and Allegro

Frederick the Great
(1712 - 1786)

Adagio and Giga

musical term

poco   **little**

new notes

E

D#

Another well-known composer of the Baroque period (1600-1750) was Archangelo Corelli. He was a virtuoso violinist and important composer. Not only was his work typical of Italian Baroque style, but he was also the creator of a new musical form known as the Concerto Grosso.

These two movements are a part of one of his sonatas written for violin. This sonata was probably one of his "sonata de camera" (sonata for the room, secular music). These sonatas were usually composed of a slower prelude plus two to four dances.

To prepare for both movements of this solo, practice the following exercise using different articulations:
1. All slurred
2. All tongued
3. Two slurred, two tongued
4. Three slurred, one tongued

PREPARATION 15

PREPARATION 16

PREPARATION 17

PREPARATION 18

The first movement, "Adagio", is slow and should be played in a lyrical, singing style and at a strict tempo.

Measures 1-6 Since you and your accompanist begin together, set the tempo and then give the downbeat. Use a light tongue throughout the movement. All notes marked with tenuto marks should be held for their full value. Observe the crescendos and decrescendos very carefully. In measure 1 two sixteenth notes are used with a dotted quarter note. Divide the last half of beat 4 into two equal parts.

PREPARATION 19

Crescendo and decrescendo the last two beats of measure 5. In measure 7 you'll see an "E♯" which is the enharmonic of "F♮", and should be fingered the same.

Measures 7-10 Play the eighth note on the last half of beat 2 in measure 7 precisely so the difference will be heard between this note and the dotted eighths and sixteenths on

the next two beats. Crescendo in measure 8 and decrescendo in measures 9 and 10 to finish the phrase. Remember that "E♯" is fingered the same as "F♮".

Measures 11-18 Beginning with the pick-up at the end of measure 10 this phrase should be "piano" until the crescendo in measure 14. Work on the octave skips in measures 11 and 12 so the lower note speaks easily.

PREPARATION 20

PREPARATION 21

Keep the embouchure relaxed on the octave skips. Put a crescendo and decrescendo in measures 14 and 15. In measure 16 make each "A" louder than the preceding one to crescendo to "forte". Close this movement "forte" with a slight ritard. on the last half of measure 17. You should cue the cut-off at the end.

musical terms

poco a poco   little by little
allarg.   gradually slower

The "Giga", the second movement, is an old dance form usually in a quick 6/8 tempo. It is also composed of wide intervals, which Corelli uses in abundance in this movement. While this was originally a rough peasant dance, it was later used as a livelier movement in concert form.

Measures 1-8   In this movement the accompaniment is in 2/4 with chords only on the beat. This should be no problem after you start with your eighth note pick-up. Your accompanist will catch the tempo from that pick-up. In measure 1 you'll notice the markings "1st time-mf" and "2nd time-p". Remember these tell you that the first time you should begin at a dynamic level of "mf" and the second time you should play "p". Watch the articulation markings carefully. All notes are to be tongued unless marked by a slur. Keep the rhythm of the 6/8 bouncy with a steady beat and a precise quarter note-eighth note pattern. When you are moving from low to high, especially in large skips, keep your embouchure firm but relaxed to help the notes speak easier. If you will also think of the melodic line as moving forward and of the pitch of the notes before you play, the continuity will remain. Each time you breathe, take a quick, big breath so the space between notes is not too big.

Measures 9-16   The second phrase begins in this measure with more emotion in the melody. Play the two eighth notes slurred followed by a staccato eighth precisely. The second slurred eighth note should be short. Diminuendo beginning in measure 10 so the crescendo in measure 13 will be more effective. This phrase will end "forte", but diminuendo slightly on the dotted quarter note "E" in measure 16 to complete the phrase.

Measures 17-33   Beginning with the pick-ups in measure 16 this phrase should be "mezzo forte" and gradually crescendo to the high "E" in measure 24. Keep the dynamic level up until measure 27. The diminuendo beginning here should be gradual until the repeat at measure 33. Repeat the first section beginning at a dynamic level of "piano".

Measures 34-41   The second section begins "forte", again with large skips in the melody. Keep your embouchure firm but relaxed when playing these skips. At measure 38 the dynamic level should be "piano" to contrast with the first part of the phrase.

Measures 42-49   The staccato notes must be short in this phrase. Begin to crescendo in measure 44. The notes marked with the tenuto should be held for their full value, and since the dynamic level is "forte", they can also be stressed slightly.

Measures 50-58   Another contrasting phrase begins here "piano" and with less movement than in the other phrases. Very smoothly connect the three-note slurs in measures 54 and 55. The crescendo will help to connect these slurs.

Measures 59-66   Begin this last phrase softly. Watch the articulation and dynamic marks very carefully. The abbreviation "allarg." tells you to grow gradually slower in measure 63 and begin to crescendo. You will give the cut-off of the last note with a small up-down motion of your instrument.

Adagio and Giga

Archangelo Corelli
(1653-1713)

Theme and Elaborations

musical terms

a tempo   in tempo, in time, return to the tempo preceding a rit.

cadenza   a section with freer rhythms played with soloist's personal inflections

new notes

B♭
(Bis)

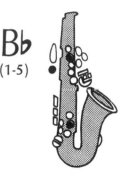

B♭
(1-5)

"Theme and Elaborations" is a contemporary composition written especially for this book. As the title suggests, it is a main theme and elaborations of that theme. It also provides an interesting study in meter, subdivision, and rhythm in a diversity of styles.

You've already studied 6/8 time signatures and you'll remember that there are six beats in a measure and an eighth note receives one beat. In this solo you'll be using 4/8, 3/8, and 2/8 time signatures in which an eighth note

gets one beat. The top number in each tells you how many beats are in a measure. Watch these changes of meter carefully as you play. In each elaboration a tempo is suggested either with metronome markings or a reference to the previous tempo.

Practice the following exercise using the different time signatures. The tempo and the note values remain the same, but the number of beats in a measure varies with the time signature.

PREPARATION 22

♪ = 76

Measures 1-8   You and your accompanist begin together so set the first tempo and then give a downbeat to begin. The main theme should be slow and lyrical at a dynamic level of "piano". Observe the nuances shown by the crescendo and decrescendo marks. Remember these are only slight changes in dynamics. Strive to make the sixteenths as rhythmic and even as you possibly can.

There are several places throughout the solo where the "B♭'s" can be played with one of many fingerings. For instance, in measures 1-8 the "B♭'s" could be fingered with the side or the "bis" key. You should choose the "B♭" fingering which is most comfortable for you. Use the side "B♭" fingering for the last "B♭" in measure 1. The "B♭" in measures 3 and 7 should definitely be fingered with the "bis" key.

"Bis" is a French word which means "alternate". In this position the first finger of the left hand closes both of the keys shown in the fingering diagram above. There are many uses for this fingering position, some of which are shown in the exercises below. Be sure that both keys are closed completely. Use a firm pressure until you get the feel of the exact place where the finger should be placed. You can keep the finger in this position while the other fingers are closing keys for the notes below. It does not affect these tones. Practice the following exercises to familiarize yourself with the "bis" fingering.

PREPARATION 23

Use "bis" fingering position throughout.

PREPARATION 24

PREPARATION 25

Measures 9-17 The first elaboration should be done at the same speed and in the same style as the theme. It is still soft, lyrical and smooth. Watch the dotted eighth-sixteenth note rhythm in measures 10 and 15. Because this movement is slow and lyrical, there should not be a noticeable space or separation between the dotted eighth and the sixteenth note. Ritard. slightly beginning in measure 16. At the end of measure 17 you'll see two slashes which are called "caesura" in Italian or "luftpausen" in German. These tell you to stop and pause before going on to the next section. The pause is also called "railroad tracks" because of the two parallel slashes. This expression is apt since you always stop at railroad tracks.

Measures 18-28 Elaboration II is faster and louder than the first two sections. The accompaniment has one measure to set the tempo. The dotted sixteenth-thirty-second note pattern must be precise throughout this section. Remember that one sixteenth note equals two thirty-second notes. The dotted sixteenth would then be equal to three tied thirty-seconds. In measures 20, 22, and 23 there is a double dotted eighth note. This note would be equal to seven tied thirty-second notes. Practice the following exercise using these two patterns. At first they are notated with tied thirty-second notes and then with dotted notation.

PREPARATION 26

♪ = 76

Only the thirty-seconds moving to the following note are slurred in this section. Watch the articulation carefully and lightly tongue the notes not marked with a slur. In measure 25 the last notes of the measure are marked with staccatos and accents so they should be short, separated, and louder than the rest of this section. Be sure to play these notes very evenly. This will bring out the contrast between the dotted notes and the straight sixteenths. The straight sixteenth note pattern appears again in the second ending at measures 27 and 28.

Measures 29-46 A time signature change occurs in Elaboration III in which there are three beats in a measure and an eighth note gets one beat. The tempo is the same as II and the accompanist helps set the feeling of three beats to a measure. This section is very song-like and smooth. Use

a legato tongue where it is necessary to put a slight separation on notes. Some vibrato should be used to enhance the singing quality of the melody. The "B♭'s" in measures 31 and 33 should be played with the "bis" key. Observe the "railroad tracks" at the end of measure 46 and pause after this section a little longer than the two beats indicated.

Measures 47-63 Elaboration IV begins with a tempo and time signature change. A new rhythm, a triplet which divides the eighth note into three equal parts, occurs in this section. ♪=♪♪♪ Practice the following exercise using the triplet with various articulations. This exercise will also give you practice using different "B♭" fingerings. Try it at the same metronome marking as this section of the solo.

The articulation in this exercise and the solo should be crisp and the staccato short, but light.

PREPARATION 27

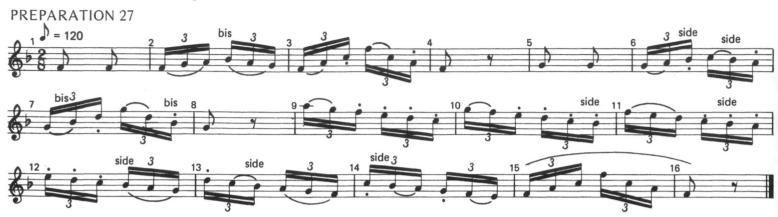

In several measures of this elaboration there are special fingerings for the "A#-Bb's" and "C's". In measures 48, 59, and 62 use the side fingering for the "Bb's" or "A#'s". For all other "Bb's" in this section the "bis" key should be easier and better to use. Any "B-C-B" movement as in measures 51, 53, and 58 should be played with the side "C" fingering. The 1-5 fingering shown above will make the "A#'s" in measure 58 easier to play.

In measure 62 the first two notes of the triplet are tied and written as one eighth note. Keep the rhythm of the triplet going in your head so you will be precise on the last note of the triplet. Watch the articulation marks in this section very carefully.

Measures 64-74 The speed of the fifth elaboration is approximately the same as the speed of the fourth elaboration. The eighth note in Elaboration IV was equal to MM=120. In Elaboration V the quarter note equals MM=63 so the eighth note is twice as fast. The composer has indicated the quarter note beat so the elaboration

would be felt in two beats even though the time signature is 4/8. This will help you feel the melody in larger groups of notes and it will be more lyrical and flowing. Watch the articulation markings carefully and use only legato tonguing. In measures 68 and 69 slur only the notes marked. On the third and fourth beats the slur is split so three of the four sixteenth notes are slurred and the fourth note begins a new slur. This articulation will cause a feeling of syncopation in these measures.

In measure 70 you have a cadenza, a section or measure which is played much freer. You'll notice there are no bar lines, but there are more than four eighth note beats in the measure. At first you may want to figure how many eighth note beats you have represented and practice measure 70 with the metronome. If this measure is broken down, it is equal to 16 eighth note beats. By studying the relationships of the groups of notes, you'll notice that the triplet figures will be faster than the eighth notes. Likewise the sixteenths would be the fastest notes of the cadenza. After you have learned the basic rhythm and the fingering patterns, you can free the rhythm.

ILLUSTRATION 6

After you play the last "B" fermata note, your accompanist has the downbeat of measure 71. This will be your cue to begin this measure at the tempo which preceded the cadenza. "Ritard" slightly in measures 73 and 74 to close-out this section.

Measures 75-93 You and your accompanist have four sixteenth notes beginning measure 75. To help start these and set the tempo for them, you should give a downbeat

cue at the tempo you will be playing. It may help to think that the tempo for this elaboration is approximately twice as fast as the previous one. The more you rehearse the solo, the more familiar you will become with the tempos.

In measure 78 use the 1-5 fingering on the "A#", the side fingering on the "C", and the side fingering on the first and second "Bb's". Practice using these fingerings in the following exercise.

PREPARATION 28

When you are playing "piano" and low notes at measure 80, be sure to keep up the breath support. Keep the sixteenth note rhythm in your mind and listen to the accompaniment so your entrance after the first beat of measure 86 will be precise. Again count carefully in measure 88 for your

entrance on the second half of the second beat. The continuous sixteenth notes of the accompaniment will be a cue for you. In measures 92 and 93 count very carefully so the last note will be exact.

Theme and Elaborations

Elaine Zajac
(1940-   )

MASTER SOLOS
INTERMEDIATE
LEVEL

Edited by Larry Teal
Performed by Elaine Zajac

Alto
Saxophone

HAL•LEONARD®

Piano (E♭ Alto Saxophone)

Intermediate Level

MASTER SOLOS
by Larry Teal

EDITED by Linda Rutherford

Contents

ISBN 978-0-7935-9549-5

Visit Hal Leonard Online at
www.halleonard.com

Contact Us:
Hal Leonard
7777 West Bluemound Road
Milwaukee, WI 53213
Email: info@halleonard.com

In Europe contact:
Hal Leonard Europe Limited
42 Wigmore Street
Marylebone, London, W1U 2RN
Email: info@halleonardeurope.com

In Australia contact:
Hal Leonard Australia Pty. Ltd.
4 Lentara Court
Cheltenham, Victoria, 3192 Australia
Email: info@halleonard.com.au

Andante and Bourrée
from
Handel Sonata No. III

George Frederic Handel
(1685-1759)

Bourrée

1st time *f*
2nd time *p*

1st time *f*
2nd time *p*

dim.

cresc.

cresc.

f

p

mf

p

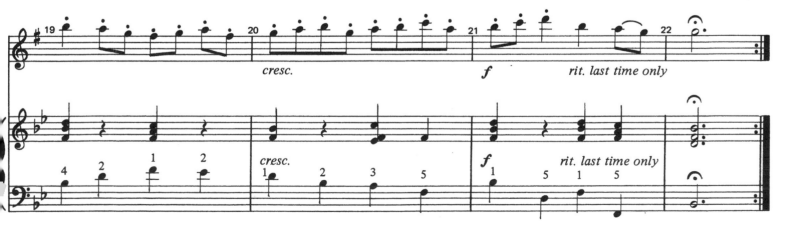

cresc.

f

rit. last time only

cresc.

f

rit. last time only

5

Adagio and Allegro

Frederick the Great
(1712 - 1786)

This Arrangement © Copyright 1975 by HAL LEONARD PUBLISHING CORPORATION, Winona, MN 55987 by Permission
Made in U.S.A.   International Copyright Secured   All Rights Reserved

Allegro

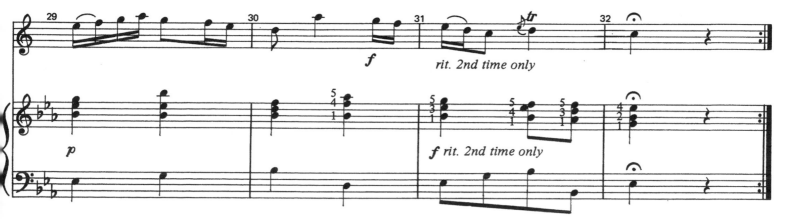

Adagio and Giga

Archangelo Corelli
(1653-1713)

Giga

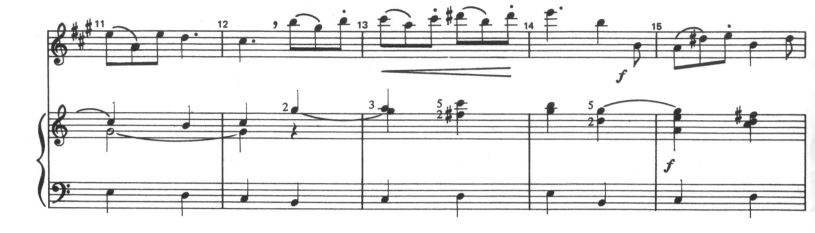

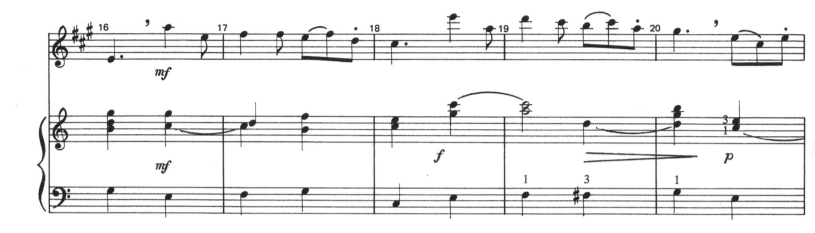

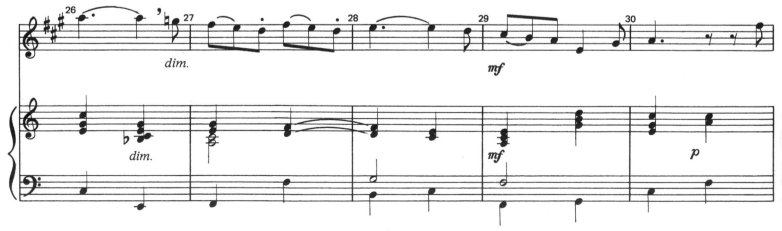

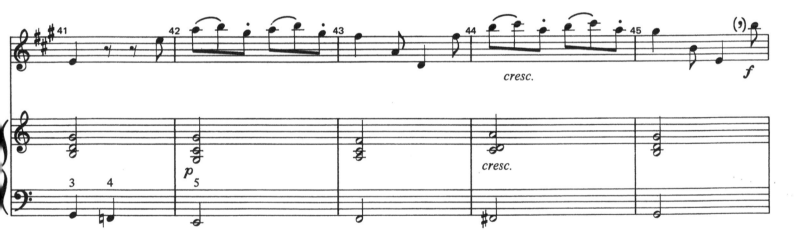

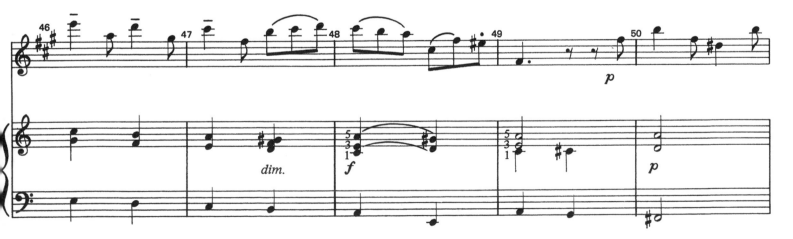

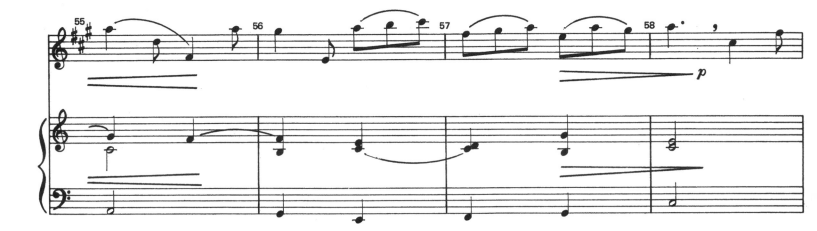

Theme and Elaborations

Elaine Zajac
(1940-   )

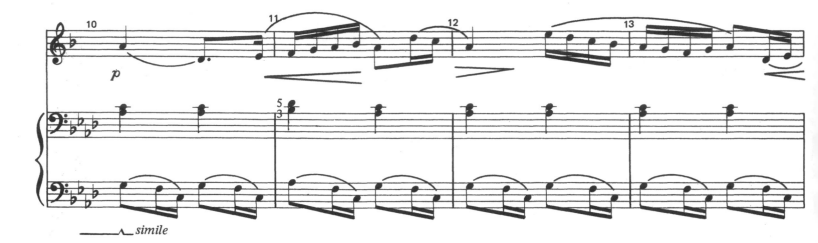

simile

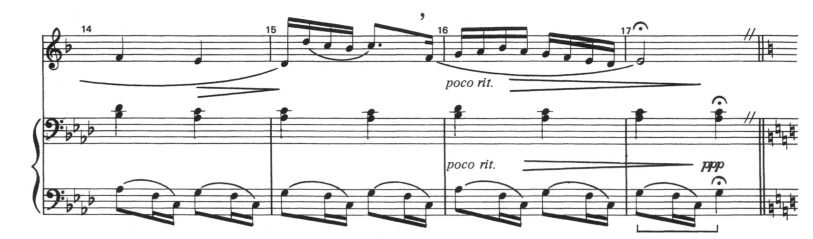

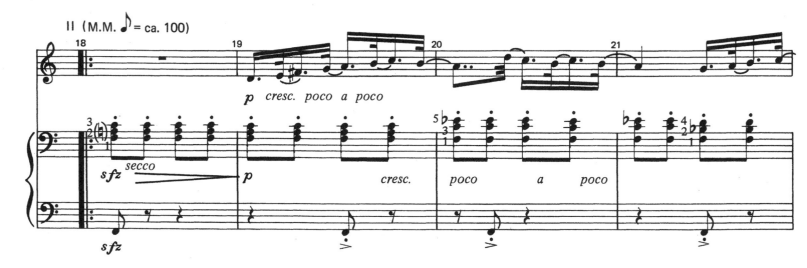

II (M.M. ♪ = ca. 100)

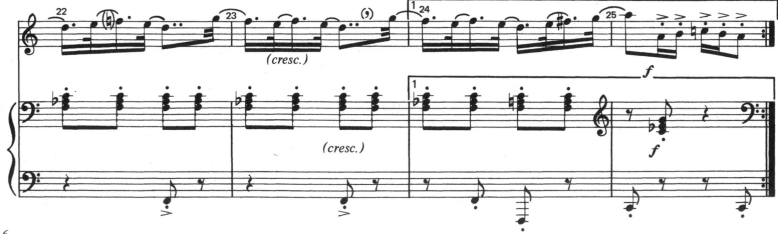

16

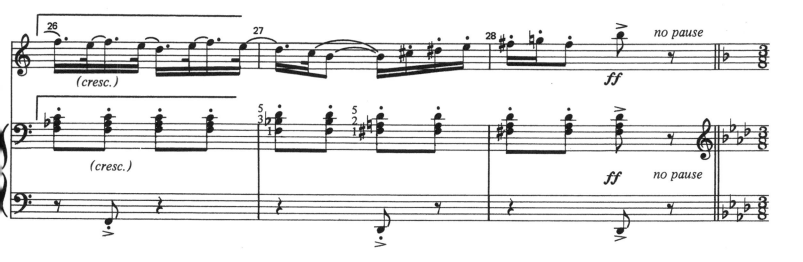

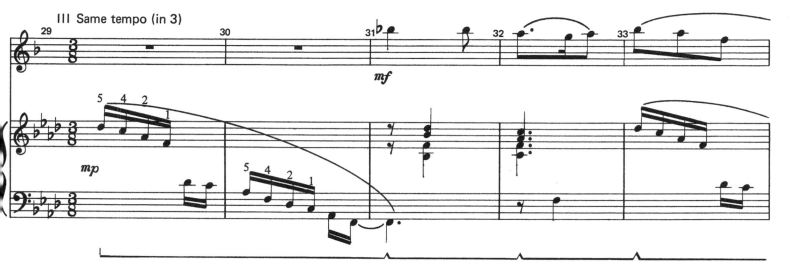

III Same tempo (in 3)

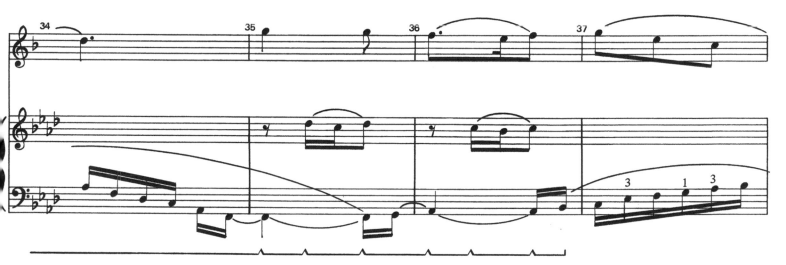

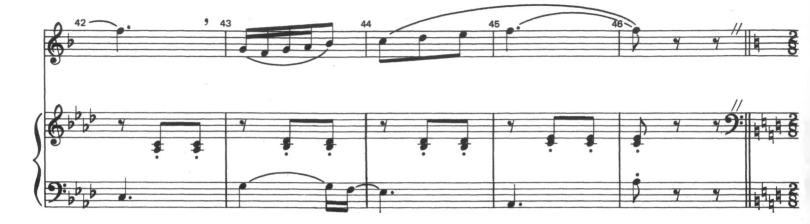

IV
Allegro (M.M. ♪ = ca. 120)

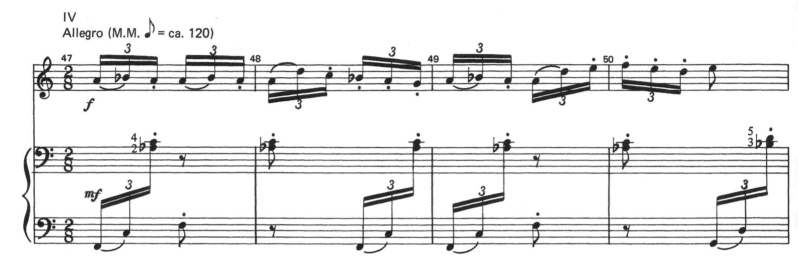

19

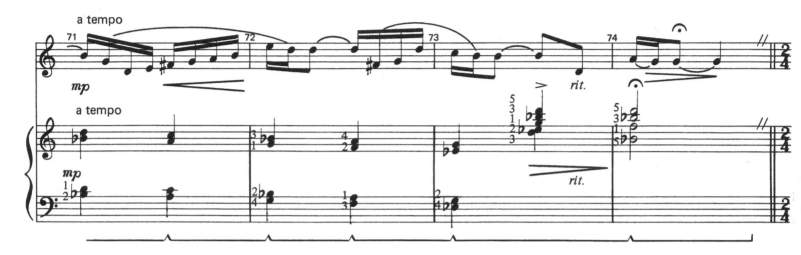

20

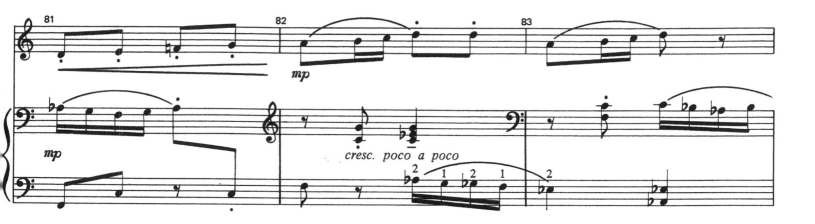

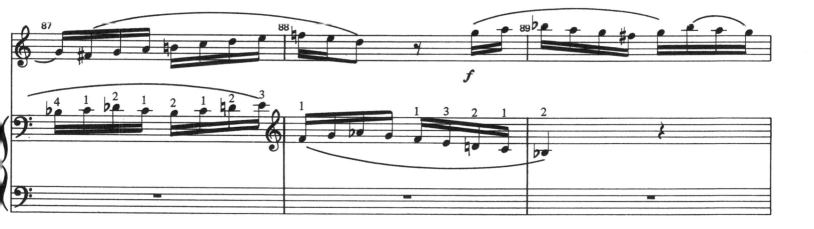

Allegro

Wolfgang Mozart
(1756-1791)

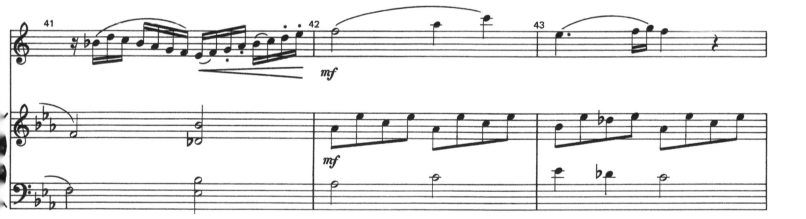

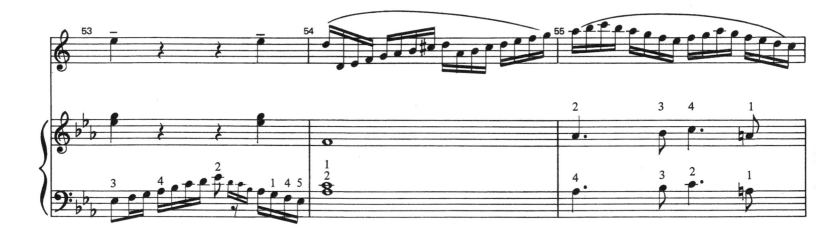

Allegro Scherzoso

Caesar Cui
(1835 - 1918)

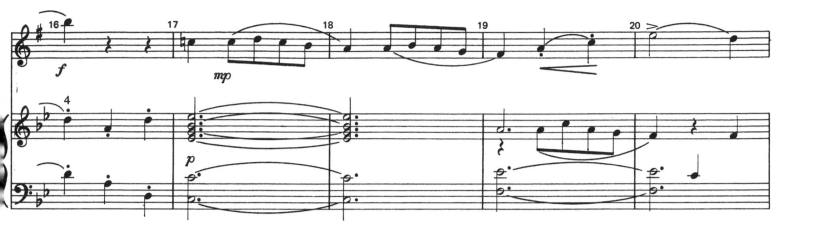

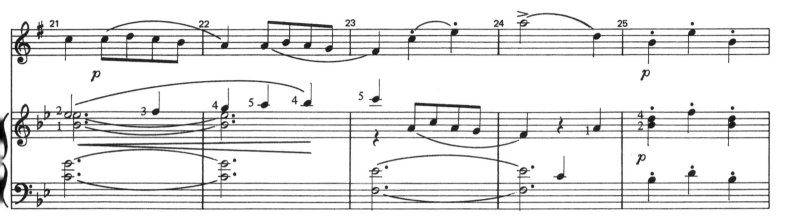

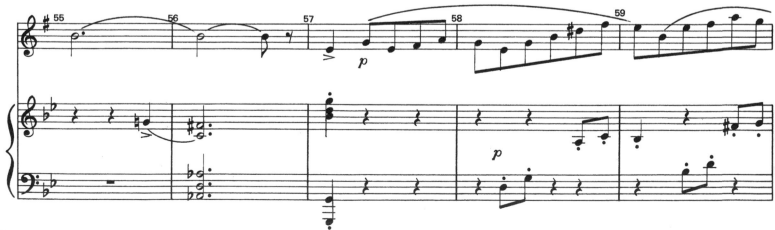

Semplice ($\flat\cdot = 52$)

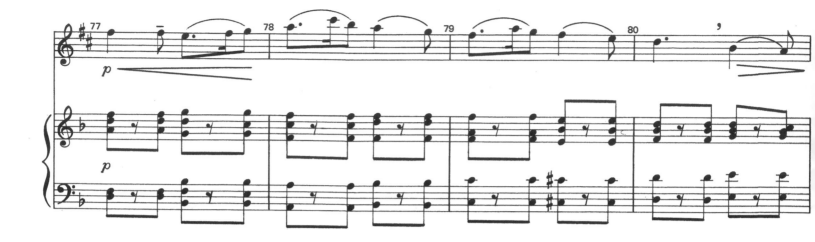

Tempo primo (♩. = 72)

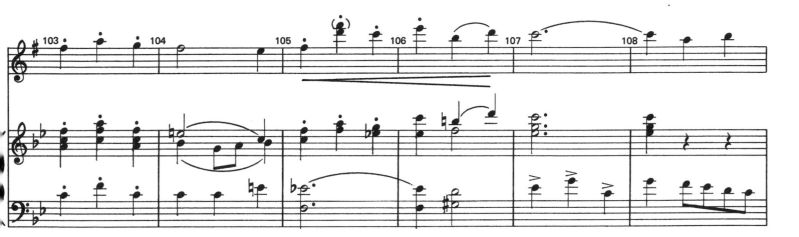

33

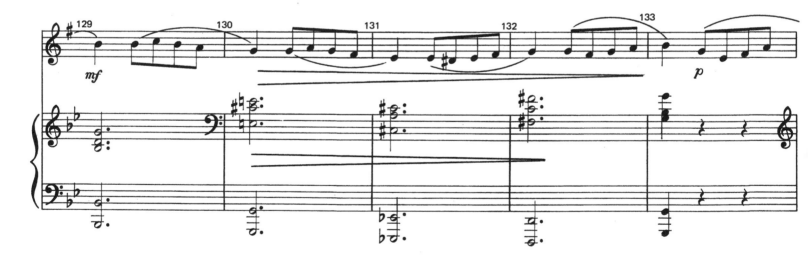

Passepied
from
Suite Bergamasque

Claude Debussy
(1862 - 1918)

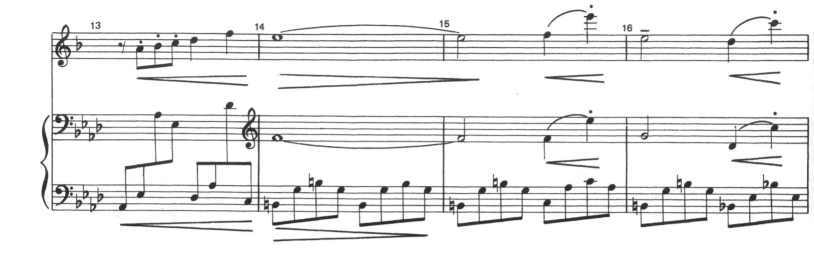

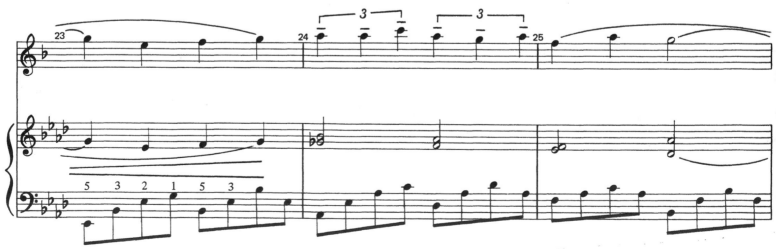

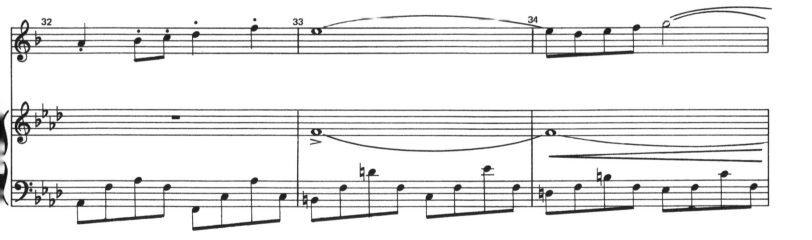

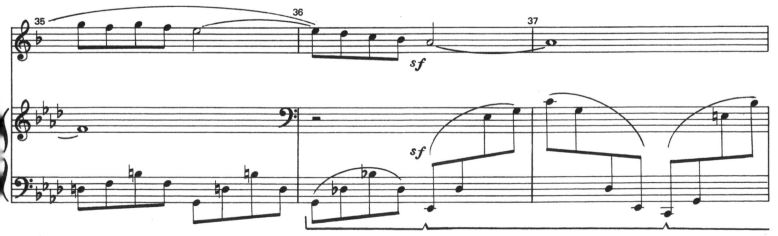

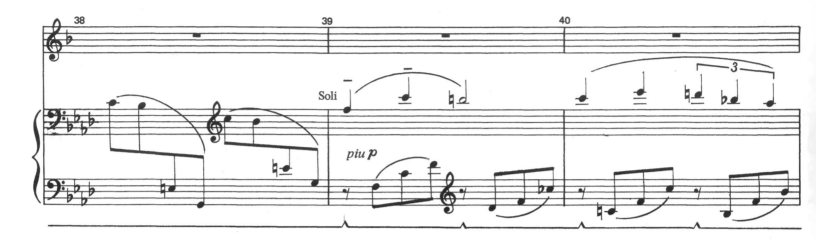

senza Ped.

39

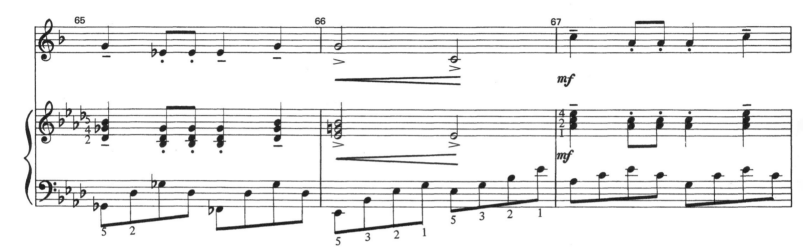

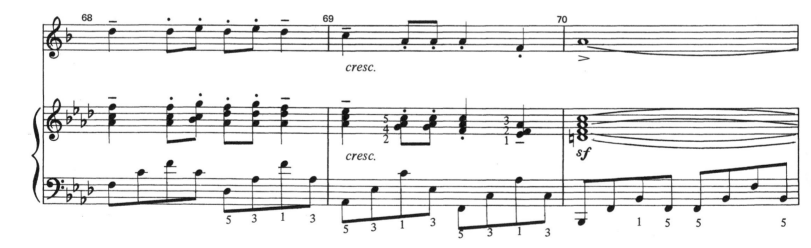

40

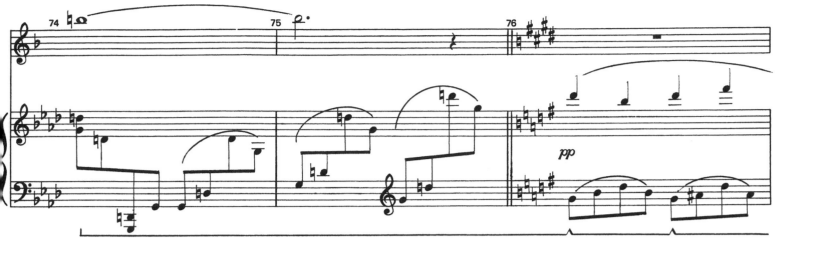

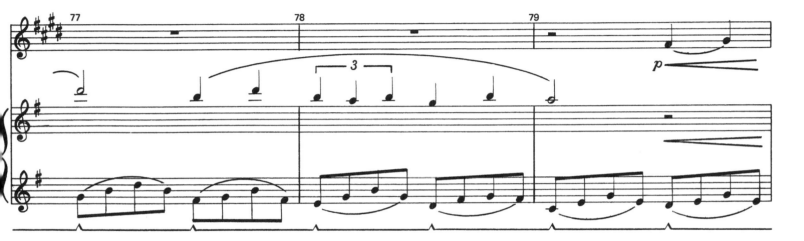

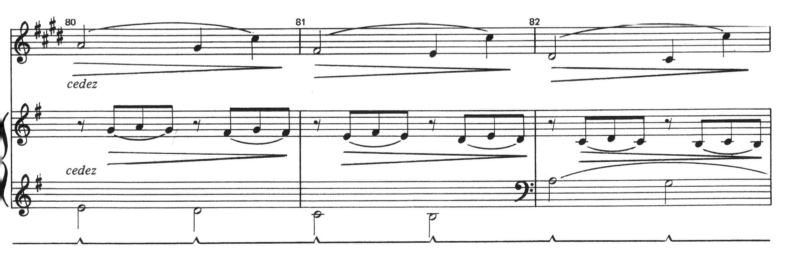

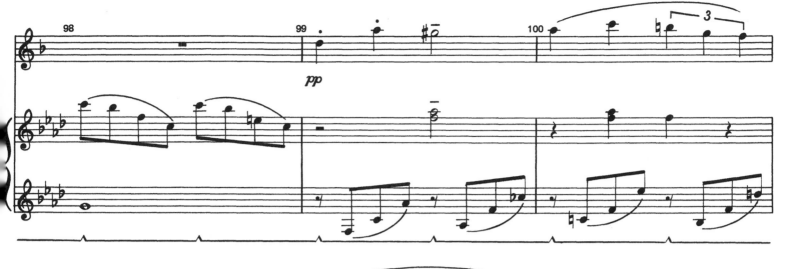

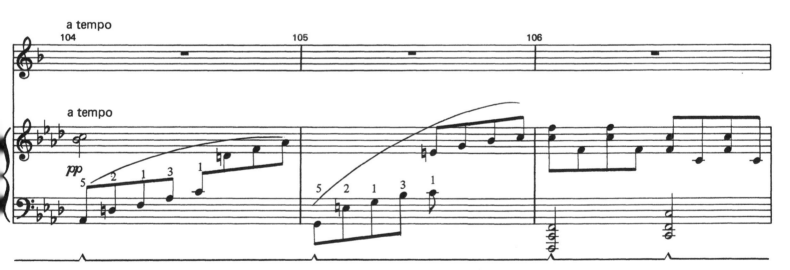

Espejos
(Mirrors)

Trent Kynaston
(1946-　　)

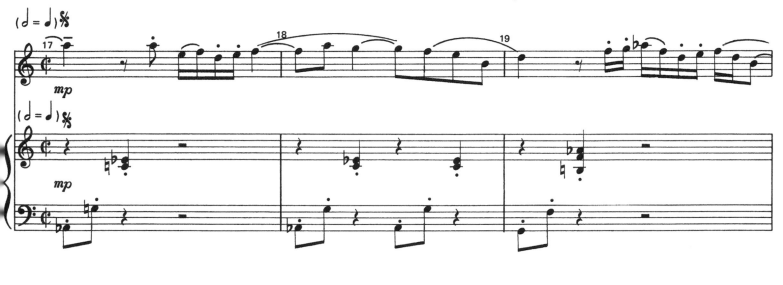

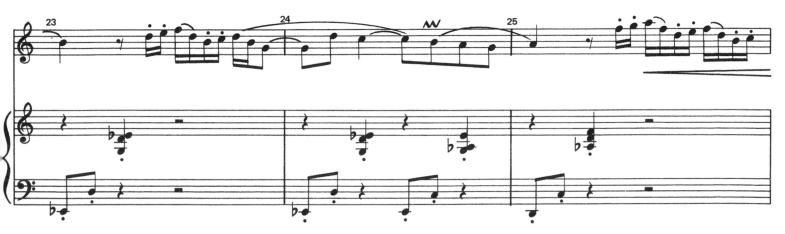

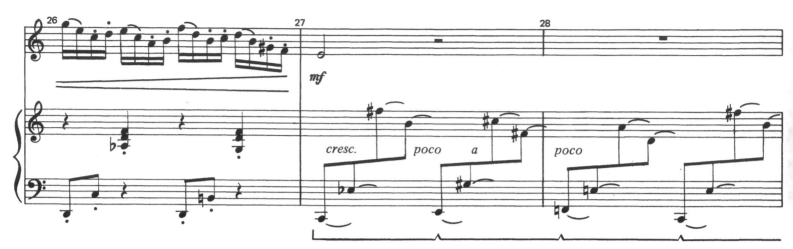

pedal simile

D.S. al Coda

D.S. al Coda

CODA
Slow - tempo primo

Allegro

musical term

dolce   sweetly

new notes

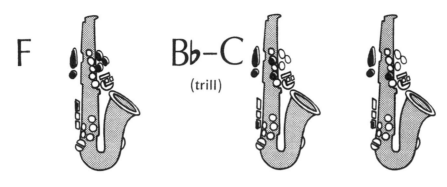

F   Bb–C
(trill)

Born in Salzburg, Austria, of a well-known musical family, Wolfgang Mozart is probably the most famous of child musicians and composers. He began studying with his father at the age of four, and by the time he was six he was performing on both the violin and harpsichord with his touring family. Mozart also started composing at a very young age, and this composition, one movement from his Sonata in C for piano was one of his early efforts. He lived only 35 years and it is difficult to comprehend how he composed so much great music in his short life.

The Classical Period (1750-1830) produced a more aristocratic musical style. The freedom of the performer to improvise was curtailed. The music is to be performed accurately and in a refined manner. The interpretation marks should be observed carefully. In general, the dynamic level in this piece should be relaxed and clear, but not too robust.

Measures 1-12   Begin the solo softly with a smooth, lyrical line. Observe the nuances (crescendos and decrescendos within melodic motives) and do not rush the sixteenth notes. The scale-like passages beginning in measure 5 are built upon the C major scale. Later in the solo other scales are used. Practice the following exercises with different articulation patterns.

PREPARATION 29
C Major

Repeat in the following articulated patterns

PREPARATION 30

PREPARATION 31

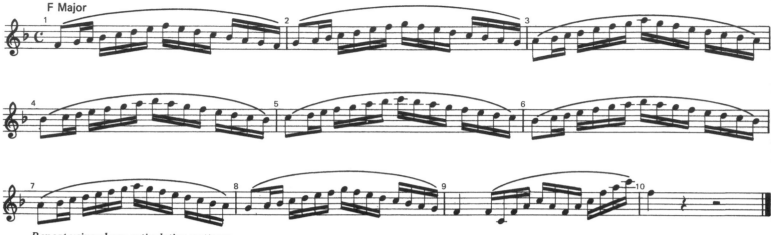

F Major

Repeat using above articulation patterns.

When you are practicing the scale exercises, strive to play with a full but relaxed breath. In measure 9 there is an optional breath mark. If at first you cannot play measures 5-12 on one breath, take a quick breath at the beginning of measure 9.

Measures 14-22 Another melodic idea is introduced here. It is lyrical and moderately soft and should be played with some vibrato. Beginning in measure 18 keep the sixteenth note pulses in your mind so each motive will begin on time and be even. The sixteenth rest in each

motive may be used to take a breath if necessary. Keep the sixteenth notes light and short.

Measures 22-28 In measure 23 the four thirty-second notes come on the second half of beat 2. Begin to crescendo on the thirty-seconds and eighths that follow, moving to the "D" in measure 24. The trill in measure 25 should begin on the upper note ("B") indicated by the small note in front of the "A". You should trill at a comfortable speed and make the notes precise and even. Practice the trill exercise slowly at first and gradually increase the speed to that of the solo. On all trills keep the trill finger close to the key. Do not raise it more than one eighth of an inch from the top of the key.

PREPARATION 32

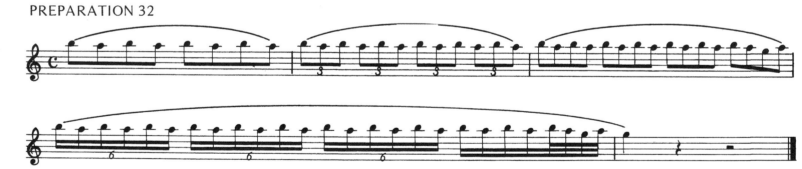

This section should always be repeated when you are performing.

Measures 29-41 Another melodic idea begins here. Watch the articulation marks very carefully so you will slur and tongue the notes as marked. Count carefully so the scale passages beginning in measure 31 are accurate. Keep the sixteenth note rhythm in mind so that this motive

begins on the second sixteenth note each time. Each quarter note of the scale should be held for its full value, but not accented. Watch the dynamics throughout this section.

Measures 42-49 The original theme is restated here with slight changes. In measure 45 the figures on beat 2 are embellished with a trill. If this were written out, it would look like the illustration below.

ILLUSTRATION 7

WRITTEN   PLAYED   or

This trill starts on the written note. Use the side "B♭"
fingering and move the first finger, left hand to trill.
Practice the trill exercise with the "B♭" to "C" fingering.

PREPARATION 33

On the scale passages beginning in measure 46 make the
crescendo and decrescendo on each measure smooth, but
do not accent the top note of each motive.

Measures 50-58 Play each tenuto with a solid, rich
tone and for its full value, but do not accent. Be sure to
take a big breath before beginning the phrase from
measure 54 to measure 58.

Measures 59-66 This is a restatement of a melodic
line that was used earlier. Remember to keep the staccatos
light and bouncy throughout the phrase and keep the
sixteenth note rhythm in your mind so your entrances
will be accurate.

Measures 67-73 In measures 67 and 68 there is a single
grace note. Remember that a grace note is a decorative
pitch usually coming before the beat. In this solo they
should be played on the beat so they would look like this
if they were written out.

ILLUSTRATION 8

The trill in measure 70 should be played like the one in
measure 25, starting with the upper note on the beat.
Practice the trill exercise using "E" and "D". Finish the
solo with a full, rich "forte" and no "ritard".

Allegro

Wolfgang Mozart
(1756-1791)

Allegro Scherzoso

musical terms

semplice   in a simple manner
tempo primo the original speed

new notes

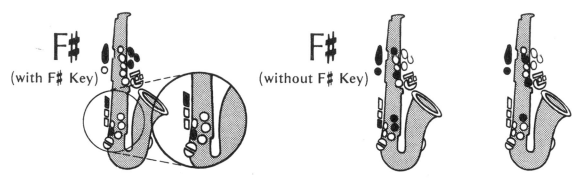

F#
(with F# Key)

F#
(without F# Key)

The Romantic period of music (1825-1900) is characterized by many developments, the most important being the pronounced individualistic styles of composers. Much of the music of this period was a part of the nationalistic schools, which used the folk music of the country as a basis for the compositions. One of the most well-known of these nationalistic schools was in Russia, propelled by a group of four composers under the guidance of Balikarev. Caesar Cui, along with Borodin, Mussorgsky, and Rimsky-Korsakov, was a member of this group. He originally was an

engineering officer and taught at the Military Academy of St. Petersburg. At the same time he was writing musical articles for newspapers of several European countries. Finally, he began to study music seriously at the age of 21. One of his most famous pieces is "Orientale", one of a group of miniatures entitled Kaleidoscope. This "Allegro Scherzoso" is also taken from this suite.

The following exercises will help you prepare for the solo.

PREPARATION 34

PREPARATION 35

Measures 1-16 The time signature for this solo is 3/4, but the metronome marking indicates that the tempo should be felt as one beat per measure. This speed makes it impractical to set the metronome at three beats per measure, but you should subdivide the beat into three equal parts in your mind. The title, "Allegro Scherzoso", tells you this is a light, lively piece, somewhat jesting in manner. You start the solo alone so get the tempo set in your mind before you begin. The accompaniment starts one measure later with the same melody. This imitation of a melody, note for note, is called a canon. This lasts from measure 1 to measure 16. Watch the dynamic and articulation marks carefully throughout. There are several places where you should use the side "C" fingering as in measures 1 and 10. Begin to crescendo slightly in measure 5 moving to the "forte" in measure 8. In measure 9 the accompaniment begins the canon melody and the soloist joins in measure 10.

In measure 15 you'll see double notes on the last half of beat 3. The high "F#" is shown in parentheses to indicate that it is an optional note and the "D" can be played in place of it. If you and your teacher decide that you should play the "F#", check the fingerings above for "F#". The two fingerings shown for instruments that do not have a high "F#" key are known as "altissimo" or "harmonic" fingerings and require special embouchure adjustment. You should discuss how to use these fingerings with your teacher.

Measures 17-40 Begin this phrase medium soft. The staccatos in measures 19 and 23 are under a slur so make these detached, but not too short. Remember to play the staccatos without slurs, short, bouncy, and crisp. Make a slight crescendo to measure 20. In measure 21 begin softly, again building to the "A" on the first beat of measure 24. In measure 37 there are double notes on beat 2. You should again decide whether to play the "F#" or "D".

Measures 41-64 The original melodic idea returns in this measure and is extended to close the first section. In measures 50 and 51 be sure to slur only the notes marked. In measure 51 the first three notes are the end of one slur and the next four notes are another slur. Accent and hold the longer notes for their full value. Again in measures 59 and 60 slur only the notes marked.

Measures 65-84 This is a simple, lyrical section and should be played softly and in an easy manner. Use little or no vibrato, and think of playing as if you were singing to yourself. To prepare for this section, practice the following exercises.

PREPARATION 36

PREPARATION 37

The speed of a dotted quarter note is slightly slower than the dotted half in the first section. You and your accompanist begin together in this section, so give the downbeat for measure 65. Since the key has changed, be sure to play "C#". Use legato tonguing on the repeated notes under the slur. The dotted eighth-sixteenth note pattern should be precise so the contrast between the sections will be noticeable. In measure 67 the grace note should be played quickly and ahead of the beat. The "D" should come exactly on beat 2.

Measures 85-100 The first section is repeated beginning here. Be sure you return to the first tempo. Accentuate the contrasts in dynamics and articulations. Remember to use the side "C" fingering on the "B-C-B" movement. In

measures 87 and 91 play the notes marked with both staccatos and a slur with a very light tongue.

Measures 101-108 In measure 105 decide whether to play the "D" or the "F#". All of the staccatos should be short and light in this section.

Measures 109-139 A repetition of the canon begins in measure 109 of the solo part. Then in measure 117 the accompaniment starts the canon and the solo follows in measure 118. Watch the articulation of measures 133 to 137. These running passages must be as smooth and even as you can make them. The last staccato should be very soft. Use enough breath support to keep the tone full and rich even at the very soft dynamic level.

Allegro Scherzoso

Caesar Cui
(1835 - 1918)

Passepied

musical terms

allegretto	light and cheerful, a little faster than moderato
piu	a little
cedez	French meaning "give way", go a little slower or play a note slightly longer
un peu	a little, slightly
sub.	suddenly

One of the most famous Impressionistic composers was Claude Debussy. He was admitted to the Paris Conservatory at age 11 where he confounded his teachers with his talent and his innovative musical ideas.

Since he lived during the Impressionistic period of music history (c. 1880-1910), his ideas were much influenced by the trend of the period. Impressionism arose as a revolt against the lush impulsiveness of the Romantic period. The artists began the movement by attempting to recapture the impression of an object or scene at a given moment. Like the poets and painters of this period, the composers wrote music that seemed to hint rather than state ideas. They in turn abandoned the typical forms of the previous periods and used a succession of colors to convey their impressions. The use of traditional harmonies was minimized and the use of exotic harmonies and folk music was increased. Much of the music of this time, especially Debussy's, was concerned with the sea, the wind, and the moonlight, as his titles usually suggest. It is not surprising that he soon became known as the father of the Impressionistic school of composition.

This solo, "Passepied", is the fourth movement of Debussy's Suite Bergamasque. Another movement of this suite,

"Clair de Lune", is probably better known. Originally a passepied was a quick, spirited dance in 3/8 or 6/8 time. Debussy retained the spirited feeling of the dance but changed the meter to cut time. The accompaniment has an eighth note figure running throughout the solo which sets the tempo. You should perform the piece with spirit and excitement, but without any roughness in the tone.

Measures 1-19 Remember that "ma non troppo" means "but not too fast", so the tempo should be lively, but not too fast. The staccatos throughout the solo should be light and crisp. Watch all of the articulation marks very closely.

Listen to the accompaniment in the first two measures to get the tempo in mind. Also prepare for your entrance in measure 3 by taking a breath and getting your embouchure set. Keep the dynamic level "piano" until the crescendo begins in measure 8. This crescendo should move toward the high "D" in measure 10. The lower "D" on beat 2 of measure 10 should be softer and the rest of the phrase should decrescendo slightly. The staccato quarter note at the end of the slur in measure 15 and other measures should be played short, but not tongued. Think of it as an eighth note followed by an eighth rest.

ILLUSTRATION 9

Measure 17 should be played a little louder (piu f).

Measures 20-30 In measure 24 there are quarter

note triplets. Earlier you learned that a triplet divided a note into three equal parts. This triplet divides a half note into three equal parts.  Try the exercises below to become familiar with this subdivision.

PREPARATION 38

The accompaniment is still playing the straight eighth note pattern. To help avoid confusion, keep in mind the two beats per measure and divide each beat into three parts.

Measures 31-37 Keep the staccatos light and crisp. Make the contrast of the eighth and quarter notes with the previous triplets noticeable. The half note on beat 2 of measure 36 is marked with a "*sf*", which stands for "sforzando" and means strongly accented. Accent this note when it begins and diminuendo slightly to round-off the sound.

Measures 38-58 With the few measures rest, draw any excess moisture from your mouthpiece as quietly as possible. Also prepare for your next entrance by taking your breath and setting your embouchure. The accompaniment has a slight ritard. in measure 43 indicated by "cedez un peu". You may need to give a small cue to begin measure 44. This measure returns to the tempo preceding the ritard. This melody is more lyrical, but don't let the tempo slow down. Use small nuances within small sections to help the melody move forward. Keep your throat open and relaxed. Watch the dynamic markings and listen to the movement of the melody line for special nuances.

Measures 59-75 The second melody of the solo is light and detached and the staccatos should be bouncy. Watch all dynamic markings carefully and emphasize the contrasts. Beginning in measure 70, crescendo to measure 75.

Measures 76-87 Use the three measures of rest to check the new key signature. This section is melodic and lyrical. When you enter, there is a ritard. indicated by "cedez". In measure 83 the tempo preceding the ritard. returns. On each diminuendo in measures 80, 81, and 82 drop back to a "mf" dynamic. Ritard. again in measure 87 before returning to the original key and the light detached melody.

Measures 88-94 Use much breath support to play the staccato short, crisp, and very soft. When the melody moves one octave higher at measure 92, it should be slightly louder and begin slowing down. The "railroad tracks" at the end of measure 94 indicate a pause of about two beats.

Measures 95-111 The accompaniment begins in measure 95 at the speed preceding the ritard. Listen to get the feel of the beat. Enter at measure 99 softly and put a slight crescendo and decrescendo in measures 99 and 100 and measures 101 and 102. During your measures of rest, prepare for your last entrance. Keep the eighth note rhythm in mind so you can enter precisely on the second eighth of measure 108. Play the last three eighth notes tongued and for their full value without any ritard. at the end.

Passepied
from
Suite Bergamasque

Claude Debussy
(1862 - 1918)

Espejos

musical term

morendo   dying away, diminuendo or decrescendo

Here is another solo composed especially for this book by Trent Kynaston. The title is Spanish for "mirrors" and the piece is exactly that, a musical mirror. The last section mirrors the beginning section, that is the beginning section played backwards. It is an atonal composition, a harmonic form that does not have a definite key or "home tone". Because of the atonality there is no key signature in the beginning, but accidentals are used in both the solo and accompaniment parts.

Measures 1-16 The tempo should be ♩=60. The accompaniment begins the solo so listen to that part, especially the third and fourth beats of measure 2, to get the tempo set in your mind before your entrance. Throughout the beginning section the dynamic level does not go above "mezzo piano". When you crescendo, "mp" should be the highest point. This first section is also lyrical and connected. Keep the basic beat steady so your entrances are precise. Remember that the "E♯" in measure 16 is the enharmonic for "F♮", so it is fingered

the same. There is also a new symbol(✗) which is a double sharp sign. You've already learned that a sharp sign raises the pitch of a note one half-step, so the double sharp raises the pitch two half-steps or one whole-step. The "F✗" in measure 16 is fingered the same as a "G".

Measures 17-28 The basic beat changes here from ♩=60 to ♩=60. Think that each beat in the first section is now equal to a half note. The articulation in this part should be light and crisp. Notice which notes are slurred and which notes are tongued. In measure 20 you'll see this sign (∿) over the "D". This is the sign for amordent, an embellishment of the written note and the scale note immediately above or below. The two illustrations below show how the mordents in measures 20 and 24 should be played.

ILLUSTRATION 10

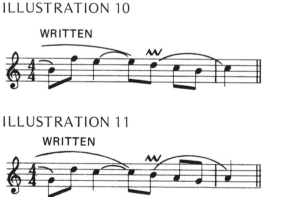

ILLUSTRATION 11

For the mordent in measure 24, use the side fingering for the "C".

Measures 30-39 There are several unusual rhythms in this section. The quarter note triplets you've already

learned in another solo. Remember to keep them even by equally dividing the beat into three parts. In measure 32 the figure on the first beat is composed of thirty-second notes tied to a dotted eighth note, so it should be played quickly on the first part of beat 1. The illustration below will show measure 32 with the counting.

ILLUSTRATION 12

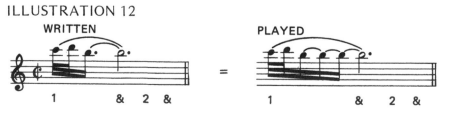

In measure 33 there is a new rhythmic figure which divides the quarter note into five equal parts and is called aquintuplet  Practice the following exercise which uses the quintuplet.

PREPARATION 40

Use the side "C" fingering and the 1-5 "Bb" fingering on the quintuplet.

ILLUSTRATION 13

Two more thirty-second note figures come in measures 34 and 35 first on the first beat and then on the second half of the first beat. Practice the following exercise to become familiar with the thirty-second figures.

PREPARATION 41

Measures 40-47 This entire section is made up of quarter note triplets and their subdivision. Strive to make them evenly and precisely divided. In measures 41, 42, 46, and 47 mordents occur within the triplets and move to the note above the written note. If there is a sharp below the mordent sign, the note to which you move should be a sharp. In measure 41 the quarter note triplet is subdivided into 6 parts. On the first note of the triplet you rest. Keep the basic rhythm in your mind so your entrance will be precise. The mordent mark with the slash in measure 43 tells you that you should play the note below the written note in the figure. Again you will be playing a "D#" because of the sharp sign below the mordent sign.

ILLUSTRATION 14

The exercise below will help you prepare for the section of triplets. Remember that the mordent sign <u>without</u> the slash means you play the upper note in the figure and the sign <u>with</u> the slash means you play the lower note in the figure.

PREPARATION 42

Remember that "E#" in measures 42 and 47 is the enharmonic of "F♮" and is fingered the same. In measure 44 you will see a "B#". This is the enharmonic for "C♮" and is fingered the same as "C". The triplet is again subdivided in measure 45 with a rest on the first part of the triplet.

Measures 17-29 Remember to go back to the sign for the repeat and play down to the coda sign at measure 30.

Measures 48-62 When you go from measure 29 to measure 48 for the coda, the tempo changes immediately back to the first tempo of the solo. Remember that the half note beat of the previous section now is equal to one quarter note. This coda section is similar to the beginning section in style — lyrical and connected phrases. Remember this is a mirror of the first part. Beginning in measure 58 it should be "piano". Be sure to take a full breath in measure 59 to last to the end. The last note should be held as long and should diminuendo as softly as possible without a break in the tone. Indicate the cut-off to your accompanist.

Espejos
(Mirrors)

Trent Kynaston
(1946-   )

fingering chart

(Notes in color are not taught in this book. Check individual solos for trill fingerings.)

B	C	C#-Db	D	D#-Eb	E	F	F#-Gb	Chromatic F#-Gb	G	G#-A

A	A#-Bb	Bis A#-Bb	1-4 A#-Bb	1-5 A#-Bb	B	C	Side C	C#-Db	D	D#-E

E	F	F#-Gb	Chromatic F#-Gb	G	G#-Ab	A	A#-Bb	Bis A#-Bb	1-4 A#-Bb	1-5 A#-B

B	C	C Side	C#-Db	D	D#-Eb	E	F	F#-Gb	F#-Gb	F#-G
								without F# Key	without F# Key	with F#